I know Jesus, he's my friend,
I talk to him each morning
as I get out of bed.

I know Jesus, he's my friend,
he rides the bus to school
with me.

I know Jesus,
he's my friend,

he watches over
me and all my friends.

I know Jesus, he's my friend,

he cheers for me at soccer
to play my best.

I know Jesus, he's my friend,
I visit him at church on Sunday
with my family.

I know Jesus, he's my friend,
I kiss him goodnight before
I go to bed.

I know Jesus, he's my friend,
he wants me to go to Heaven
and live with him.